WORD MASTERY

WORD MASTERY

A COURSE IN PHONICS FOR THE FIRST THREE GRADES

BY

FLORENCE AKIN

Teacher in Primary Grades, Pasadena, California

ISBN: 978-93-5128-783-4(HB)

First Published in 1913
Indian Reprint in 2017

Published by

Kalpaz Publications
C-30, Satyawati Nagar,
Delhi – 110052
E-mail: kalpaz@hotmail.com
Website: kalpazpublications.com
Ph.: +91-9212142040

PREFACE

This little book is intended to be put into the hands of children at the beginning of their first year in school. It may be used in conjunction with any series of readers.

Teachers generally recognize the value of a good foundation in phonics as an important aid in learning to read. Unfortunately many teachers are not sufficiently familiar with the principles underlying phonic analysis and the building of words to feel sure that they can make their phonic drills as economical and as effective as they should be. Pupils, therefore, often fail to get sufficient phonic practice to become proficient in word recognition. Moreover, no matter how helpful the readers may be in suggestions as to teaching phonics, it devolves upon the teacher to prepare a great deal of phonic work. This requires much time and energy, as it must of necessity be presented to the pupils from the blackboard, or from large printed cards and charts. It has seemed to the author that it would be a great advantage to both teacher and pupil to have before the pupil in a book a carefully worked out and thoroughly tested series of exercises in phonics, which have been found to make pupils self-reliant in word mastery.

The author has evolved this system of teaching phonics in her own schoolroom, and has found that it ensures rapid progress in learning to read. It is presented to her fellow teachers with the hope that it may serve to lighten their burdens, and bring to them greater success in the fine art of teaching reading.

M m

Do not undertake to teach these lessons until you have carefully studied the "Suggestions to Teachers," page 110.

M, n, r, f, s, l represent sounds that may be prolonged. **This makes them the easiest of the consonant sounds to blend, and therefore to learn first. See directions on page 111 for teaching the sound of *m*.**

A a

N n

man

Pupils can now "build" the word *man:* they should first sound the word and then tell it. See page 111.

R r

ran

Pupils should learn to tell tne number of each page as they go over it. This will enable them to turn for review to any page required.

F f

fan

S s

Sam

E e

men
man
fan
Sam
ran

ran
man
men
fan
Sam

Take each step slowly at first. Lay the foundation well.

T t

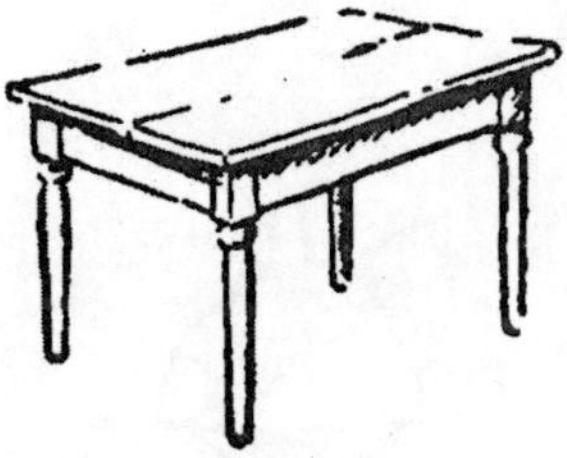

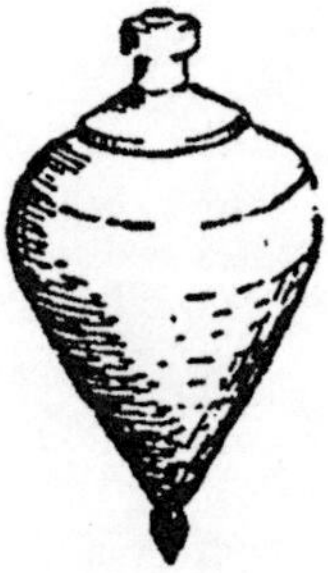

mat	set	ten
met	sat	tan
Nat	rat	
net	fat	

T, used first as a terminal, then as an initial sound.

L l

let

G g

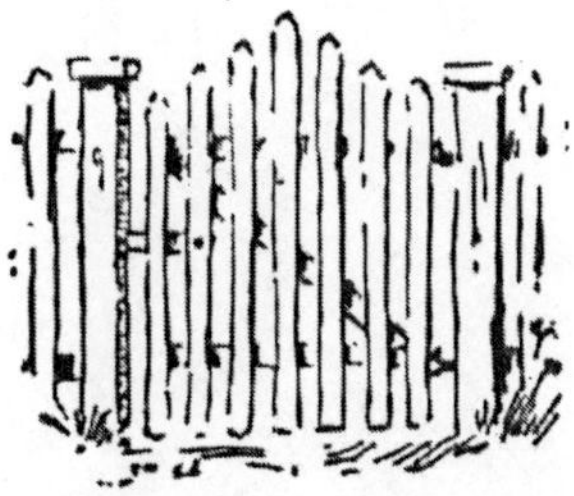

rag	gas
tag	get
sag	gag

G, used first as a terminal, then as an initial sound.

C c

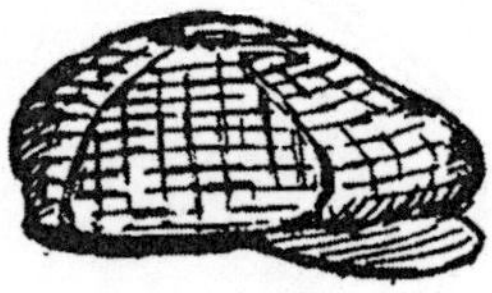

cat
can

can
cat

K k

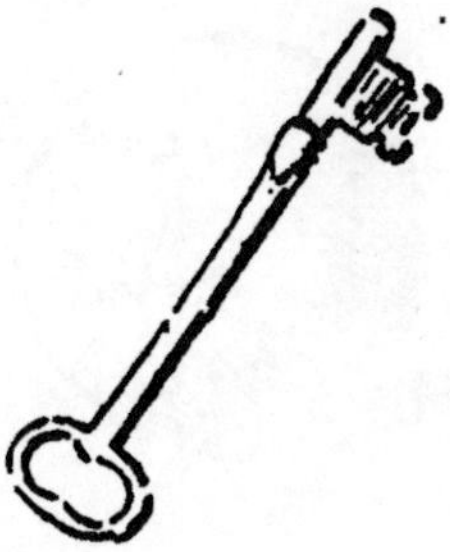

keg

B b

cab	Ben	bag
Tab	bat	beg

I i

bit	tin	bib
bat	ten	big
sit	tan	beg
sat	fit	bag
set	fat	fin
fig	rib	rim

These pages require much patience and care.
Go slowly now, and speed will come later.

H h

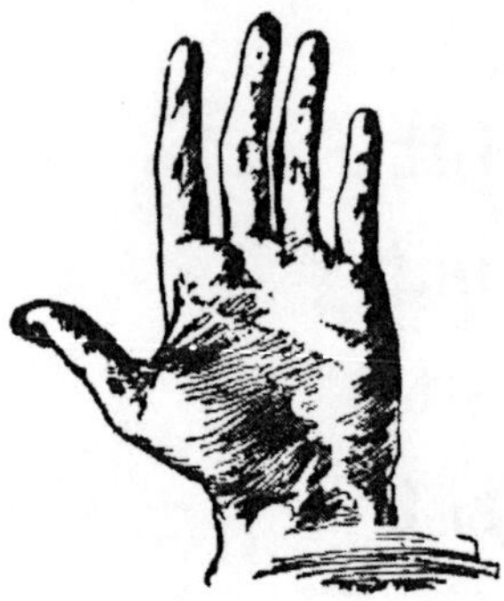

hat	**hem**	**him**
hit	**ham**	**hen**

D d

red	hid	sad
rid	had	did
lad	mad	den
led	mid	din
lid	bed	dig
fed	bad	dim

P p

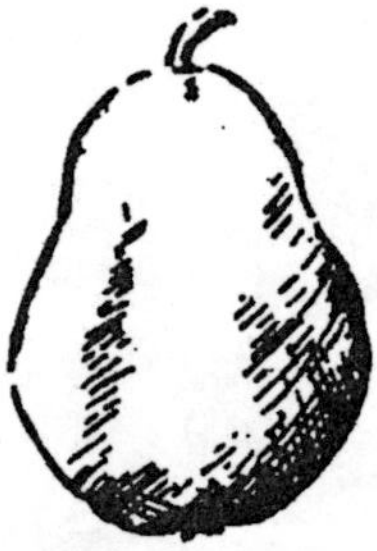

tap
tip
rip
rap
sip
sap
nap

map
lap
lip
cap
dip
hip
pan

pin
pen
pet
pat
pit
pig
peg

O o

log
fog
fig
cob
cab
rob
rib
nod
sod
pod
pad

rod
rid
red
hop
hip
lap
lip
lop
top
tap
tip

got
pot
pat
pet
pit
hat
hit
hot
let
lot
dot

J j

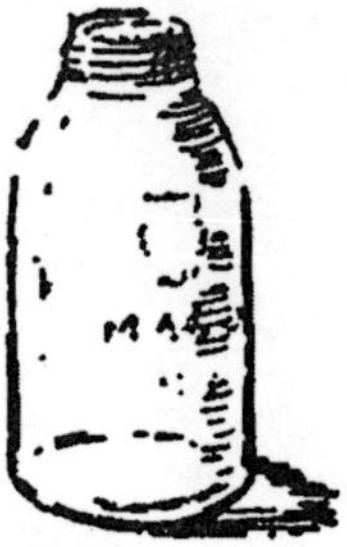

jam

jet

W w

wag wit web
wig wet win

U

u

gum
hum
hem
ham
him
bug
beg
bag
big
rag
rug
hug
jug

pug
peg
pig
tag
tug
tub
hub
rub
mud
bud
sup
cup
pup

run
bun
Ben
fun
gun
sun
cut
hut
hat
hot
hit
but
nut

Z z

X x

ax

box

six

x = ks

Q q

V

vat

van

v

van

vat

Y

y

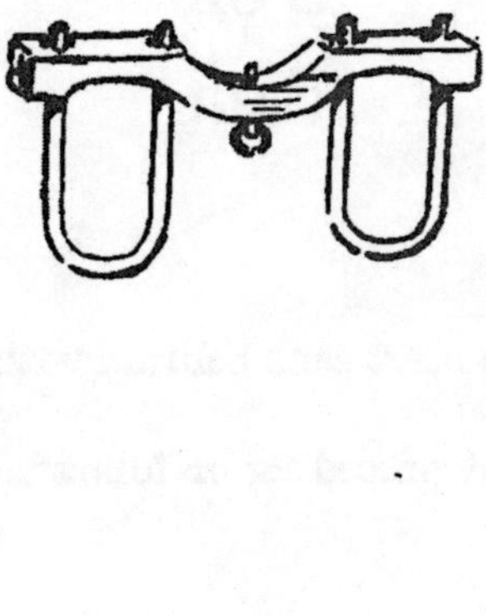

yes

yet

yet

yes

a	e	i
at	n et	it
c at	p et	b it
b at	g et	h it
h at	l et	s it
s at	w et	w it
m at	s et	f it
p at	m et	p it
r at		
	h en	in
an	m en	p in
c an	p en	t in
f an	t en	s in
m an	B en	w in
p an	d en	f in
r an		

Be sure that pupils start each column with the short sound of the vowel.

Only one consonant preceding or following the vowel.

o	u	a
d ot	c ut	c ap
h ot	n ut	l ap
l ot	b ut	m ap
p ot	r ut	n ap
c ot	h ut	g ap
t ot		s ap
n ot	s un	t ap
g ot	g un	r ap
	f un	
h op	r un	b ad
m op	b un	h ad
p op		m ad
t op	up	s ad
l op	c up	p ad
s op	p up	l ad
	s up	

e	i	o
r ed	h id	p od
l ed	d id	r od
f ed	l id	n od
b ed	m id	s od
N ed	b id	
	k id	h og
h em	r id	l og
		f og
b eg	d ip	
l eg	h ip	c ob
k eg	l ip	r ob
p eg	r ip	m ob
	t ip	s ob
w eb	p ip	
	s ip	ox
R ex		b ox
v ex		f ox

u	a	i
b ud	am	h im
m ud	j am	r im
	h am	d im
g um	S am	
h um		b ig
	t ag	d ig
b ug	b ag	p ig
r ug	w ag	f ig
h ug	r ag	w ig
m ug	s ag	j ig
j ug		
p ug	c ab	b ib
t ug	T ab	r ib
t ub	ax	s ix
r ub	w ax	f ix
h ub	t ax	m ix

an	c an	f an
at	c ap	f at
am	c ob	f ed
ax	c ot	f ig
	c ub	f in
b at	c up	f it
b ad	c ut	f og
b ag		f ox
b ed	d en	f un
b ig	d ip	
b it	d id	g as
b ox	d ig	g et
b ug	d im	g ot
	d ot	g um
c ab	d in	g un
c at	d ug	

This review is to strengthen the pupils' knowledge of consonant sounds.

h at	j am	m en
h ad	j et	m et
h am	j ug	m ix
h en		m ud
h id	k eg	
h im		n ap
h ip	l ad	n et
h it	l ap	n ot
h op	l et	n od
h og	l ed	n ut
h ot	l ip	
h ug	l id	on
h um	l og	ox
h ut		
	m an	p an
if	m ad	p at
it	m ap	p eg
in	m at	p en

p et	s et	up
p ig	s in	us
p in	s it	
p od	s ix	v an
p op	s ob	v at
p ug	s od	v ex
	s un	
r ag		w ag
r ed	t ag	w ax
r im	t an	w eb
r ip	t ap	w et
r ob	t ax	w ig
r ug	t en	w in
r un	t in	
	t ip	y es
s ad	t op	y et
s ag	t ub	
s ap	t ug	z ig z ag

can	let	tip
bit	pat	sad
ham	Tom	wax
let	beg	peg
Dan	rug	mix
lip	Nan	tub
rod	rap	box
beg	map	log
fed	bed	cab
sit	fig	hem
did	rob	red
tag	vex	big
lid	jug	keg
mat	rib	bat
Ben	top	ten
run	cup	led

General review without separating the phonograms.

The foundation is now laid. If the work has been well done, success is assured.

Short — a e i o u

Long — a e i o u

at	c an	S am
ate	c ane	s ame
h at	p an	m ad
h ate	p ane	m ade
m at	m an	f ad
m ate	m ane	f ade
r at	c ap	h id
r ate	c ape	h ide
f at	t ap	d im
f ate	t ape	d ime

Teach the words *long* and *short* as whole or "sight" words. Practice sounding the vowels at the top of the page — both long and short.

Final e is silent and usually makes the preceding vowel long.

f in	b it	l op
f ine	b ite	l ope
p in	r id	n ot
p ine	r ide	n ote
t in	r od	c ut
t ine	r ode	c ute
w in	r ob	us
w ine	r obe	use
d in	h op	t ub
d ine	h ope	t ube
r ip	m op	c ub
r ipe	m ope	c ube

a

w ade
s afe
b ake
r ake
c ake
l ake
w ake
m ake
t ake
g ale
p ale
s ale
t ale
c ame
g ame
n ame

l ame
t ame
J ane
l ane
b ase
c ase
v ase
K ate
d ate
g ate
l ate
c ave
g ave
p ave
s ave
w ave
g aze

i

s ide
w ide
t ide
l ife
w ife
m ile
p ile
t ile
f ile
l ime
t ime
m ine
l ine
v ine
n ine
w ipe

Long vowel sounds.

k ite
f ire
m ire
w ire
t ire
h ire
f ive
h ive
d ive
l ive

o
p oke
j oke
y oke
p ole
h ole
m ole

s ole
b one
c one
t one
l one
r ope
h ome
d ome
c ore
t ore
s ore
w ore
m ore
d ose

no
go
so

u
t une
J une
Luke
Duke
p ure
c ure
m ule
m ute

e
he
be
we
me

late	hive	home
mine	mane	cape
gave	rate	date
bite	tine	robe
pole	yoke	Duke
cane	pane	dive
wire	pile	fade
dime	more	gate
hope	ride	rode
pure	tire	vane
wore	pipe	hire
line	lake	ate
bone	pine	June
rake	ripe	cake
wove	tone	rope
time	life	vase

Review of long vowel sounds without separating the phonograms.

core	wake	hole
kite	Kate	tame
make	side	wine
same	lame	Luke
safe	note	tape
vine	Jane	wipe
sale	cure	bale
pale	wave	mule
vote	size	pave
sake	use	name
made	nine	bake
lone	mate	here
wade	cave	came
case	take	tune
dose	wide	fore
save	gaze	tide
fate	wife	cone
hide	lane	tore

c at	c ake	r akes
c ats	c akes	r ats
		m akes
c ap	g ate	w ipes
c aps	g ates	j okes
		b akes
s it	p ipe	t ips
s its	p ipes	d ates
		c ups
d ip	b ite	w akes
d ips	b ites	k ites
		w ets
t op	r ope	h opes
t ops	r opes	t aps
		f its
n ut	y oke	p ets
n uts	y okes	m aps

Showing the *s* form of words.

s = z	g ames	b ox es
as	t unes	s ix es
h as	r ose	h ose
is	r os es	w ise
h is	n ose	r ise
p ins	n os es	r is es
l ids	ax es	m ix es
r ugs	t ax es	f use

Ned's cap	Ben's cup
Kate's rose	Sam's bat
Tom's cane	Ted's dime
Jane's cake	mule's rope
Dan's fox	cat's bed
Dave's home	hen's leg
Nat's box	man's gun
Bob's top	pig's pen

S often has the sound of *z*, as in the first exercise. The second exercise shows the possessive form of words.

b ack	b ell	l ess
l ack	f ell	B ess
p ack	s ell	h iss
s ack	t ell	k iss
t ack	w ell	m iss
d eck	N ell	f uss
n eck	ill	m uss
p ick	b ill	
l ick	f ill	b uff
k ick	h ill	r uff
t ick	k ill	c uff
s ick	m ill	m uff
l ock	t ill	p uff
r ock	w ill	
b uck	d oll	f uzz
d uck	d ull	b uzz
l uck	h ull	

When two consonants having the same sound come together, only one is sounded.

an d
h and
l and
s and
b and

en d
b end
m end
s end
w ind
p ond

b ent
r ent
s ent
t ent
w ent

h int
l int
m int
t int
h unt

b est
n est
t est
w est
r est
v est
l ist
f ist
m ist

d ust
m ust
r ust
j ust

c amp
d amp
l amp
l imp
r omp
b ump
d ump
j ump
l ump
p ump

s elf

Two different consonants following the vowel.

b elt	g ift	el k
f elt	l ift	m ilk
m elt	r ift	s ilk
w ilt	s ift	b ulk

h elp	k ept	n ext
y elp	w ept	t ext

---

left	send	hand
huff	tilt	sift
hemp	hint	lend
went	west	hiss
less	romp	held
Jack	Bess	add
Jill	wick	Bell
next	pump	dent
mock	Dick	Bill

The second exercise is a review.

ch

ch ime
ch ick
ch oke

ch in
ch ap
ch ase
ch eck
ch ill
ch afe
ch ip
ch at
ch op
ch ose
s uch
m uch
r ich
b en ch
l un ch
b un ch
p un ch

p atch
l atch
c atch
h atch
m atch
itch
w itch
p itch
h itch
d itch
n otch
b otch
D utch

New sound — *ch.*
T is silent before ch.

sh

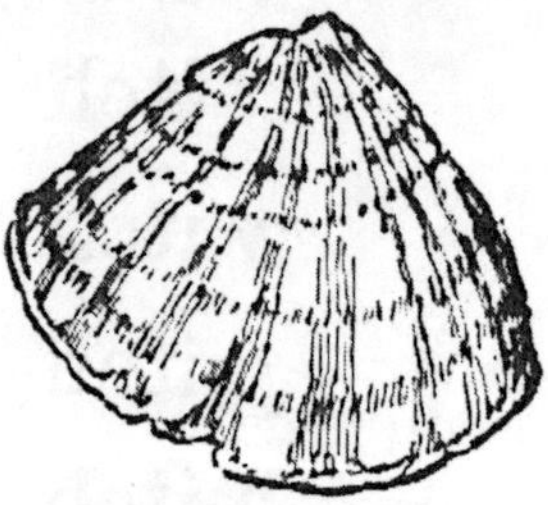

sh ade
sh ake
sh all

sh ame
sh ape
sh ed
sh ell
sh elf
sh ine
sh ip
sh ock
sh od
sh one
sh ot
sh ore
sh op
sh un
sh ut
sh ave

a sh
c ash
d ash
l ash
m ash
s ash
d ish
w ish
f ish
h ush
r ush

sh r ub
shr ill
shr imp
shr ed
shr ug

New sound — *sh.*

th

th in
th ick
th ump

w id th
t en th

th r ill
thr ob
thr ive
thr one
thr ash
thr ush
thr ust
thr ift

th e
th at
th en
th is
th ese
th ose
th em
th us
th ine
th an

w ith
b athe

On this page are two new sounds — the voiced and the voiceless sound of *th*. It is often necessary for a pupil to sound the word both ways in order to discover the correct pronunciation.

wh

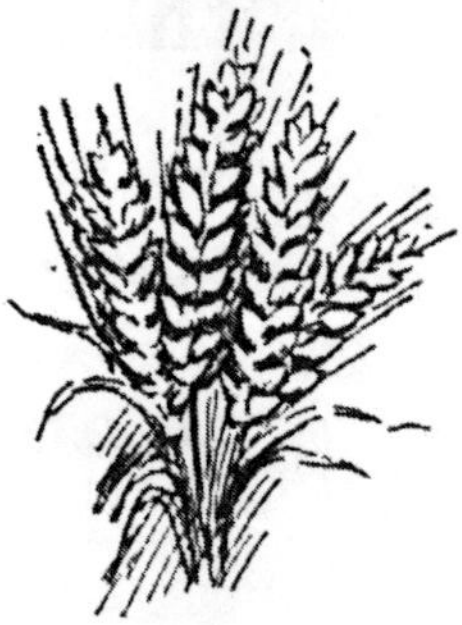

wh ip
wh ale
wh en
wh et
wh ich
wh ine
wh iff

wh ile
wh ack
wh ite
wh im
wh iz

---

shake
thatch
chores
which
shift
this

chill
mush
whine
with
shade
these

shuck
chop
then
chest
thrush
shrill

First exercise shows a new sound — *wh*.
Second exercise is a review of *ch*, *sh*, *th*, and *wh*.

bl	pl	cr	gr	sm
cl	sp	sc	pr	sn
fl	sl	dr	tr	sw
gl	br	fr	st	tw

---

bl ack	cl ick	fl ag
bl ade	cl ock	fl ake
bl ame	cl uck	fl ame
bl aze	cl am	fl at
bl ed	cl ap	fl ax
bl ess	cl ip	fl esh
bl ock	cl od	fl it
b lot	cl ose	fl ock
bl uff	cl ub	fl op
bl unt	cl utch	fl ash
bl ush	cl ove	fl ume

Consonant combinations. Pupils should practice blending the two consonants so closely that they form but one sound.

gl ad	sp ade	sl ack
gl ade	sp an	sl ab
gl aze	sp eck	sl ash
gl ass	sp ell	sl am
gl ide	sp end	sl at
gl obe	sp ill	sl ate
	sp in	sl ave
pl an	sp ine	sl ed
pl ant	sp oke	sl ip
pl ate	sp ot	sl id
pl ot	sp un	sl it
pl um	sp ike	sl im
pl ume	sp ire	sl ime
pl ush	sp ite	sl ide
	w isp	sl ope
s pl ash	l isp	sl ush
spl it		sl ug
spl int		

br an
br ag
br ake
br ave
br ick
br ide
br im
br oke
br ush
br ine

cr ab
cr ack
cr ate
cr ane
cr op
cr amp
cr isp

cr imp
cr ept
cr ib
cr ush
cr ock
cr ust

s cr ap
scr ape
scr atch
scr ub

sc amp
sc at
sc ale
sc ant
sc ore

sc um
Sc otch
sk ate
sk etch
sk iff
sk ill
sk ull
sk ip
sk im
sk in

r isk
br isk
h usk
d usk
m usk
t usk

dr ag
dr ess
dr ift
dr ill
dr ive
dr op
dr ove
dr ug
dr um
dr ip
dr ape
dr one

fr ame
fr et
fr esh
Fr ench
fr ill

fr og
fr ock
fr om
fr isk
fr oze

gr ade
gr and
gr aze
gr ate
gr ave
gr ape
gr ip
gr it
gr ill
gr in
gr ove
gr unt

pr ess
pr ide
pr ize
pr op
pr ose
pr int

s pr ig
spr ite

tr ack
tr act
tr amp
tr ash
tr ap
tr ade
tr ick
tr ill

tr im	st ab	st one
tr ip	st ack	st op
tr od	st ake	st ub
tr ot	st ale	st uck
tr uck	st amp	st uff
	st omp	st ore
s tr ip	st ump	h aste
str ipe	st and	p aste
str ive	st ate	t aste
str etch	st ep	w aste
str ict	st em	b aste
str ide	st ick	cr est
str ike	st iff	ch est
str ap	st ill	l est
str oke	st ilt	bl est
	st itch	cr ust
	st ole	tr ust
	st ove	

sm ell
sm elt
sm ash
sm ile
sm ith
sm oke
sm ack

sn ake
sn ap
sn atch
sn iff
sn uff
sn ipe
sn ore
sn ug
sn ag

sw am
sw ell
sw ept
sw im
sw um
sw ine
sw itch
sw ore
sw ift

tw ig
tw ill
tw ine
tw ist
tw it
tw itch
tw ins

qu

qu ack
qu ill
qu ilt
qu it
qu ite
qu iz
qu ick

s qu int

New combination — *qu*.

blend	crust	clamp
stripe	trade	sprig
broke	frame	scrape
fleck	twist	risk
slide	spend	flap
stitch	grim	snatch
drape	quench	scamp
smile	fluff	splash
print	skate	swift

---

d og	cr oss	l ost
off	gl oss	fr ost
l oss	l oft	m oth
t oss	s oft	fr oth
m oss	c ost	cl oth

First exercise is a review.

The vowel sound in the lower list of words differs slightly from the short sound of *o*. Webster's New International Dictionary gives it a mark indicating a medial sound between that of the *o* in *orb* and the *o* in *odd*. Special care should be taken to give pupils the correct pronunciation of these words.

y es	p up py	**y = long i**
y et	c ar ry	by
y ell	emp ty	my
y elp	d ust y	cr y
Y ale	tw en ty	dr y
y oke	f if ty	fl y
	s ix ty	fr y
y = short i	n ine ty	pr y
c and y	c op y	sl y
ch er ry	fl uff y	sp y
m er ry	f un ny	th y
w ind y	j ol ly	tr y
k it ty	f og gy	wh y
p en ny	B et ty	r ye
ch ill y	H en ry	sh y
s or ry	B un ny	sk y
s un ny	P ol ly	st yle

Three sounds of *y*.

ai	**sail**	**pain**
ay } = **long a**	**snail**	**lain**
ai d	**pail**	**plain**
l aid	**tail**	**slain**
m aid	**trail**	**chain**
	aim	**stain**
paid	**claim**	**faint**
braid	**gain**	**paint**
ail	**rain**	**quaint**
fail	**drain**	**raise**
bail	**brain**	**praise**
rail	**grain**	**waist**
hail	**train**	**bait**
jail	**strain**	**gait**
mail	**sprain**	**wait**
nail	**main**	**strait**

When two vowels come together, the first is usually long and the second silent.

b ay
d ay
r ay
tr ay
g ay

gray
hay
lay
clay
may
pay
play
say
stay
stray
way
pray

ea, ee = long e

s ea
t ea
fl ea
ea ch
b each

peach
reach
teach
bead
lead
read
leaf
leak
beak
peak

speak
weak
streak
sneak
squeak
heal
meal
seal
squeal
steal
beam
seam
team
steam
stream
dream
bean
lean

mean
clean
heap
leap
cheap
reap
ear
fear
hear
near
tear
dear
year
clear
shear
ease
easy
tease

please
east
beast
feast
yeast
eat
beat
heat
meat
neat
seat
cheat
treat
wheat
eaves
leave
heave
weave

see
fee
bee
flee
free
glee
three
tree
beech
leech
speech
screech
deed
feed
need
seed
weed
bleed

reed	screen	meet
greed	keen	sheet
beef	queen	sweet
reef	green	street
seek	sheen	fleet
week	deep	greet
cheek	keep	breeze
creek	sheep	freeze
meek	steep	sneeze
eel	sweep	squeeze
feel	creep	
heel	sleep	**ie = long i**
keel	peep	d ie
peel	deer	l ie
reel	cheer	
steel	queer	fie
seem	beet	pie
seen	feet	tie

oa } =long o oe }	groan	coast
	loan	boast
l oad	moan	
r oad	soap	t oe
t oad	oat	w oe
l oaf	coat	
c oach	float	hoe
	goat	foe
poach	boat	
roach	throat	ue = long u
oak	oar	s ue
cloak	soar	c ue
croak	roar	
soak	board	hue
coal	coarse	due
goal	hoarse	
foam	roast	
roam	toast	

long i

m ild

wild
child
bind
blind
find
hind
kind
mind
wind
grind

igh = long i

s igh
s igh t
fight
might
high
light
night
right
tight
bright
flight

long o

old
t old
cold
gold
hold
mold
sold
scold
roll
toll
stroll
post
most
colt
jolt
bolt
pork
torn
worn
porch
forth
both

I* is long when followed by *ld, nd,* or *gh.* *O* is long when followed by *ld.

ow

ow l
h owl

fowl
scowl
growl
bow
brow
cow
how
now
plow

mow
down
town
gown
clown
frown
crown
brown
drown
crowd
drowsy

ou = ow
c ouch

crouch
pouch
slouch

loud
cloud
proud
bound
found
mound
pound
round
ground
sound
wound
count
mount
our
sour
scour
flour
house

mouse
grouse
blouse
out
pout
spout
sprout
stout
trout
shout
mouth
south

ow, ou = long o

owe
bow
low
blow
flow
row
grow
glow
crow
mow
show
snow
throw
stow
bowl
own
mown
sown
blown
grown
flown
thrown
growth
yellow
window
elbow
hollow
mellow
widow
shadow
four
pour
court
course
soul

ing ings

k ing	matting	singing
k ings	running	bringing
r ing	boxing	fretting
r ings	rubbing	trying
s ing	mixing	braiding
s ings	packing	playing
	filling	reading
string	puffing	meeting
sling	buzzing	loaning
wing	bending	lighting
wings	hunting	folding
swing	resting	rolling
spring	jumping	plowing
springs	helping	counting
bring	adding	flowing
cling	wishing	pouring
thing	spending	minding
things	throwing	steering

er ers

h er	rubber	crackers
w ere	deeper	brighter
j erk	temper	Easter
n erve	pitcher	miller
	hammer	grinder
perch	timber	counter
fern	roller	sleeper
verse	rollers	teacher
ever	thunder	owner
stern	older	owners
term	colder	sifter
sister	dinner	browner
sisters	rocker	gayer
flower	painter	bitter
flowers	painters	upper
winter	wilder	tender
winters	summer	singer
better	cracker	servant

skip	lye	sketch
creek	please	snow
grain	leaf	grape
might	swell	roller
mint	perch	slush
soak	bill	night
mine	sling	totter
cream	beet	failing
roaring	foggy	gray
chase	graze	prize
owe	ore	woe
fright	power	laid
bunch	howl	saying
snail	told	rose
spring	fear	board
flyer	meaning	rain
speak	ground	waste
strike	lost	thrown

General review.

flesh	blade	Jack's
bone	socks	leader
shift	drugs	snake
supper	mopping	froth
trust	stretch	post
sorrow	sand	whiz
perch	peach	cores
off	patter	thrush
four	glad	stand
suppose	clinch	plump
clings	bench	twine
greedy	weaker	blister
cloth	offer	June
follow	scolding	shelf
jail	west	wetter
spins	flock	sweep
coal	shaggy	pills
smear	house	wades
raise	still	throat

slope	smile	twelfth
feeds	toss	dray
stake	study	oaks
cheese	splash	frills
tinner	street	coats
times	shadow	cherry
swept	snatch	saves
cheek	trout	frosty
trench	crust	feelers
ever	vote	lamp
fish	stitch	preach
shells	kind	sleeve
bluff	twig	toast
sniffs	clerk	May's
tried	sweets	crown
teeth	pepper	style
wing	brain	teams
hack	close	pillow
cost	mouse	breeze

ang ong ung eng

bang	song	sung
hang	songs	stung
hanger	gong	swung
rang	prong	slung
gang	strong	sprung
gangway	tongs	strung
clang	hung	length
sprang	rung	strength

---

n=ng	thanking	think
bank	drank	blink
blank	sank	sunk
clank	tank	chunk
plank	ink	trunk
rank	link	trunks
crank	mink	stronger
Frank	pink	hunger
Frank's	sink	hungry
thank	drink	angry

making	raising	trading
grading	spading	striking
skating	sloping	stroking
waving	closing	framing
hiding	blazing	blaming
riding	taking	flaming
smiling	mining	scraping
chiming	storing	whining
shining	lining	bathing
stoning	freezing	thriving
driving	squeezing	shaving
smoking	pleasing	choking
hoping	leaving	chasing
curing	weaving	taming
wading	praising	siding
piling	wasting	filing
raking	tasting	snoring
draping	pasting	hiring

Final *e* is dropped when *ing* is added.

kn = n

knob
knot
knee
kneel
knit
knits
knife
know
knows
known
knight
knead
kneads
kneading
knack
knock
knocks
knocking

wr = r

wrap
wraps
wren
wrench
wrenches
wring
wringer
wringing
wrist
wrists
wrong
write
writes
writing
wrote
wreath
wreck
wrecks

mb = m

lamb
lambkin
limb
comb
climb
dumb
crumb
numb
plumbing
thumb

gn = n

gnat
gnats
gnash
gnashes
sign
signboard

gu = g	league	buys
guess	leagues	buyer
guesses		buying
Guy	**bu = b**	
guide	build	**bt = t**
guides	builds	doubt
guiding	builder	doubts
guest	building	doubting
plague	built	debt
rogue	buy	debts

---

wrist	wrench	doubt
comb	gnat	guest
guess	writes	wrong
build	know	knock
debts	guide	gnash
buy	kneel	dumb
wreath	limb	knot

The second exercise is a review.

matting	pinning	holly
mating	pining	holy
lopping	dinner	latter
loping	diner	later
filling	mopping	hopping
filing	moping	hoping
slopping	shamming	batting
sloping	shaming	bating

---

happy	planning	blotter
ladder	supper	cracker
bonnet	yellow	rabbit
motto	begging	carry
summer	shabby	hammer

A vowel is short when there are two consonants having the same sound *between it and* the next vowel.

napkin	velvet	public
silver	lifting	mending
pilgrim	pumpkin	pitcher
candy	sister	dentist
dustpan	renting	picnic
number	trumpet	melting
window	slender	empty
camping	crusty	thunder

---

story	smiling	zero
closing	pupil	cozy
baker	pony	hero
duty	sober	tiger
navy	tulip	tiny
solo	lady	gravy
fever	clover	paper
music	shady	hazy

A vowel is short when there are two or more different consonants between it and the next vowel, and long when there is but one consonant between it and the next vowel.

There are frequent exceptions to this rule, yet it is helpful.

ai = short i

captain
fountain
mountain

ea = long a

break
breaks
breaker
breakers
breaking
daybreak
great
greater
steak
beefsteak

ea = short e

head
dead
read
ready
dread
dreads
lead
bread
spread
thread
deaf
breast
health
healthy
wealth
wealthy
meant
feather
leather
weather
heavy
sweat
breath
meadow

ie = long e

chief
thief
thieves
brief
field
priest
tier
wield
yield
shield
grief
grieve
grieves

ed	crowded	waded
petted	sifted	seated
landed	folded	pouted
faded	clouded	roasted
tested	boasted	handed
needed	tended	doubted
twisted	rented	coasted
wicked	jolted	mended
tinted	graded	weeded

ed = d	peeled	soured
sailed	frowned	buttered
played	foamed	roared
kneeled	crowed	wheeled
mired	breathed	scattered
plowed	pinned	shivered
aimed	prayed	cleaned
loaned	climbed	snowed
growled	sealed	canned

ed=t	wrecked	kissed
reached	liked	guessed
puffed	wrapped	dropped
baked	stamped	coaxed
clapped	leaped	checked
ticked	dressed	shipped
brushed	knocked	scraped
patched	wrenched	dashed
choked	packed	milked

---

mounted	skated	sighed
battered	grunted	painted
rusted	wretched	lacked
cried	begged	mailed
floated	ailed	kicked
pained	mixed	rained
strayed	tacked	heaped
cracked	missed	lighted

The second exercise is a review of phonograms. The words *are new.*

ie, ey = short y		
	kitties	sixties
	daisies	carries
Annie	stories	berries
Jimmie	candies	copies
Bessie	ponies	pansies
Hattie	ladies	bunnies
Jessie	pennies	donkey
Lizzie	empties	chimney
Nellie	fifties	alley
Willie	puppies	valley

---

ei, eigh, ey = long a		
	reign	weight
	eight	sleigh
	eighteen	neigh
skein	eighty	freight
reins	eighty-five	they
reindeer	eighty-six	greyhound
veil	eighty-eight	whey
vein	weigh	prey

boot

oo
o
u
ou
ui
ew

} like long oo in boot

too	gloom	loose
hoof	gloomy	broom
roof	soon	root
proof	moon	hoot
cool	noon	shoot
pool	spoon	boost
tool	teaspoon	choose
stool	loop	coo
spool	looped	coop
food	droop	scoop
room	stoop	scooped
boom	hoop	groove
bloom	goose	poor

book

oo
o
oul
u

like **short** oo in **book**

good
good-bye
hood
childhood
stood
understood
wood
woods
woodpile
woodshed
cook
cooking
hook
fishhook
shook

took
undertook
look
looked
brook
brooks
crook
crooked
foot
wool
wolf
wolves
could
would
should

put
putting
puss
push
bush
bushes
cuckoo
butcher
pudding
puddings
pull
pulling
pulled
pulpit
full

ful	truthful	playful
cheerful	painful	plentiful
thankful	fretful	healthful
dreadful	frightful	restful
powerful	fearful	useful
tearful	bashful	hopeful
spiteful	hateful	shameful
helpful	grateful	doubtful

---

boy

oi, **oy** } like **oy** in **boy**

	coin	toy
	join	Roy
oil	joint	joy
toil	point	enjoy
soil	moist	joyful
boil	noise	oyster
spoil	noisy	boyhood

apple
cattle
saddle
tumble
candle
thimble
steeple
cuddle
puddle
tinkle
pickle
tangle
kettle
maple
bottle
beetle
cradle
wiggle

handle
eagle
tremble
bundle
brittle
middle
people
table
ruffle
crackle
stumble
wrinkle
single
dimple
bugle
needle
stable
riddle

battle
buckle
paddle
twinkle
pebble
rumble
settle
crumble
shingle

tle = l

thistle
wrestle
whistle
bristle
nestle
rustle
trestle

T is silent in *tle* after *s*.

c = s before e, i, y

ice
rice
mice
nice
slice
price
twice
face
lace
place
space
race
trace
brace
Grace

fence
quince
since
Prince
Alice
ounce
bounce
flounce
cell
center
cease
piece
niece
fierce
voice

choice
grocery
ceil
pencil
city
cider
cinders
icicle
juice
juicy
spice
spicy
cyclone
bicycle
Lucy

***C* before *e*, *i*, or *y* has the sound of *s*.**

g = j before { e, i, y }		dg = j
		badge
		Madge
gem	fringe	edge
age	plunge	ledge
gage	Roger	hedge
sage	gentle	wedge
rage	huge	sledge
stage	college	pledge
cage	gill	dredge
page	engine	ridge
range	ginger	bridge
change	gingerbread	dodge
strange	magic	lodge
stranger	Gyp	budge
danger	Egypt	nudge
manger	gypsy	judge
hinge	dingy	

***G* before *e*, *i*, or *y* usually has the sound of *j*.**

ly

safely
gaily
fully
sadly
gladly
lightly
slowly
poorly
loudly
kingly

slyly
nicely
softly
likely
daily
badly
freely
swiftly
quickly
lonely
mostly

gently
kindly
lately
truly
bravely
neatly
nearly
wholly
closely
ugly
boldly

---

less

blameless
aimless
wireless
useless
homeless
fearless

tasteless
tireless
lifeless
painless
hopeless
boundless
matchless

shameless
priceless
endless
senseless
thankless
restless
speechless

ness
sweetness
meanness
kindness
illness

stillness
lameness
thickness
weakness
loneliness

soreness
sadness
sickness
goodness
happiness

---

est
coldest
nicest
loudest
lightest
slowest
kindest
tamest
safest
tightest
ripest
wildest
sweetest

lamest
dampest
sorest
stiffest
wisest
latest
finest
lowest
oldest
widest
dearest
brightest
roundest

reddest
softest
crossest
gladdest
grandest
biggest
nearest
blackest
newest
stillest
thickest
freshest
happiest

ar
ear
ir } = **er**
or
ur

lantern
desert
finger
rooster
every
flutter
spider
beggar
cedar
dollar
backward
earn
learn

search
earth
heard
pearl
bird
chirp
girl
first
skirt
birthday
shirt
stir
dirt
fir
firm
squirm
third
whirl
squirrel

thirty
circle
thirsty
word
work
world
worm
worse
worst
worth
stubborn
flavor
tailor
sailor
doctor
neighbor
bur
fur
blur

sturdy	nurse	burst
urge	churn	purple
curl	burn	church
curly	turn	turtle
hurl	hurt	further
purse	curve	nursery

---

ish	foolish	stylish
dish	finish	Irish
wish	polish	Spanish
fish	selfish	British
rubbish	punish	furnish

---

butterfly	sunbeams	himself
grapevine	sunset	firefly
raindrops	sunrise	fireside
rainbow	cobweb	midnight
dewdrops	forget	windmill
sunshine	blackboard	daylight

Third exercise is a review of phonograms, with new words.

star

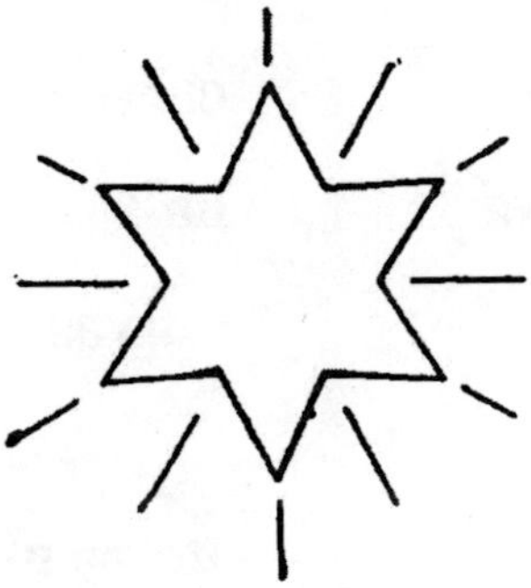

a } like a in star
au }

	starlight	lark
	starch	arm
bar	starve	farm
marble	hard	harm
march	yard	harmless
arch	bark	charm
car	dark	barn
card	darkness	darn
scar	mark	yarn
far	park	art
jar	parlor	artist
tar	spark	tart
star	sparkle	cart

When *a* and *r* come together, if *a* does not follow a vowel, their sound is usually the name of the letter *r*.

(The exceptions are in such words as *war*, page 94.)

dart	grandpa	lf = f
part	grandma	calf
party	father	calves
chart	grandfather	half
start	aunt	halves
startle	jaunt	
large	launch	lm = m
charge	craunch	calm
sharp	laundry	calmly
harvest		palm

---

chair

ar
air
ear
eir
ere

} like air in chair

care	carefully	carelessly
careful	careless	carelessness

careworn
dare
daring
fare
farewell
bare
barefoot
threadbare
hare
spare
square
squarely
rare
rarely
rarest
ware
hardware
glare
glaring

flare
snare
stare
share
shared
scare
scarecrow
scarce
scarcely
air
airy
fair
fairy
fairest
hair
hairbrush
pair
armchair
stair

staircase
stairway
bear
grizzly bear
polar bear
pear
tear
tearing
wear
wears
their
theirs
ere
there
therefore
where
wherever
nowhere
elsewhere

saw

a, **aw**, **au**, **augh**, **o**, **ough** — like **aw** in **saw**

all
almost
ball
baseball
call
fall
hall
tall
wall
walnut
stall
small
salt

lk = k
walk
sidewalk
talk
chalk
stalk

war
warble
warm
warn
warning
swarm

wharf
quart
quarter
wigwam
water
want
jaw
gnaw
law
claw
paw
hawk
draw

straw	caught	corner
strawberry	taught	scorn
thaw	daughter	horn
awl	or	thorn
scrawl	order	north
squaw	border	torch
awning	for	scorch
shawl	nor	sort
dawn	cord	short
lawn	cork	morn
yawn	horse	morning
fault	form	orchard
saucer	storm	ought
cause	stormy	bought
gauze	fork	brought
pause	stork	fought
haul	New York	sought
author	born	thought
Paul	corn	nought

ough = long o	although	doughnut
though	dough	borough

---

basket

a as in basket

	after	master
	afterward	past
	rafter	path
ant	ask	bath
grant	task	branch
slant	mask	brass
chance	clasp	class
dance	grasp	glass
glance	cast	grass
France	fast	mass
raft	last	pass
draft	blast	chaff
craft	mast	giraffe

a = short o

was	watchful	waffle
swan	what	waffles
wand	wash	wallow
wander	washing	swallow
wanderer	washboard	swallows
wandering	washtub	swamp
wasp	whitewash	swamps
wasps	squash	swampy
watch	wad	quality
watchman	wads	quantity

---

o, ou, oo = short u

son	won	wonderfully
grandson	wonder	none
ton	wonderful	done

some	sponges	smother
somebody	tongue	smothered
somebody's	tongues	oven
somehow	front	govern
something	month	dozen
sometime	nothing	London
sometimes	cover	young
somewhat	covered	younger
somewhere	color	wondrous
come	colors	serious
coming	colored	touched
love	comfort	trouble
lovely	other	southern
loveliest	others	double
above	another	country
shove	mother	countries
dove	mother's	couple
gloves	grandmother	flood
sponge	brother	blood

half-long a	damage	savage
furnace	bandage	Sunday
necklace	cottage	Friday
surface	voyage	Thursday
package	courage	Tuesday

---

half-long e	beyond	relief
became	deceive	recess
before	decide	receive
begin	delay	recite
began	delight	rejoice
begun	deliver	reply
behind	declare	recover
belong	depend	pretend
behave	desire	preserve
below	despair	prefer
between	select	erase
besides	secure	cement

Unaccented vowels. To discover the words, pupils should sound these vowels long. Familiarity with the spoken word will enable them to make these vowels more or less obscure.

half-long o	protect	factory
oblige	provide	memory
obey	propel	daffodil
disobey	profess	evaporate
polite	produce	tobacco
provoke	ivory	November

half-long u	capture	gesture
unite	lecture	venture
united	furniture	pasture
future	moisture	century
picture	mixture	failure

obscure a	amid	around
ago	alone	away
awoke	asleep	astray
adrift	alike	about
afloat	afraid	aloud

Second exercise — **When *t* precedes half-long *u*, together these letters form a more or less clear *ch* sound.**

Third exercise — To discover the words, pupils should sound *these* and the following obscure vowels like short *u*.

arise	India	Cinderella
along	China	umbrella
soda	collar	salad
sofa	lizard	spectacles
Clara	manager	climate

---

obscure a	instant	disappoint
real	servant	appear
medal	giant	disappear
loyal	currant	balloon
royal	vacant	account
final	lilac	errand
crystal	arrange	balance
several	Scotland	arrest
hospital	Holland	madam
emerald	fisherman	allow
distant	German	breakfast

The sound of *a* in the lower exercise differs slightly in pronunciation from its sound in the preceding exercise. hence these two sounds are offered in separate groups.

obscure e	flannel	present
jewel	vessel	agent
cruel	gravel	silent
camel	level	absence
angel	travel	mitten
barrel	satchel	passenger
towel	bushel	hello
chisel	moment	children

obscure o	consent	cannon
commence	connect	seldom
complete	content	blossoms
complaint	contain	bottom
welcome	console	parrot
tiresome	lion	pilot
handsome	melon	gallop
confess	lemon	occur
concern	lemonade	offend
conclude	ribbon	conductor
control	wagon	hammock

obscure u	subtract	sirup
suppose	circus	stirrup
suggest	Saturday	
succeed	album	

---

en } = **n**	kitten	**ten = n**
in } = **n**	sweeten	glisten
on } = **n**	maiden	often
	sudden	soften
golden	basin	listen
open	raisin	hasten
chosen	button	
broken	cotton	**el = l**
frozen	season	ravel
seven	reason	mantel
given	lesson	tassel
stolen	poison	shrivel
widen	prison	

In the second exercise there are elided vowels. They may be presented to the pupils as silent.

dismiss	invent	excite
disgust	invite	excel
dislike	interrupt	exercise
dispute	engage	except
display	enemy	excuse
distress	entire	explode
divide	entirely	explain
direct	enter	extreme
impure	unload	express
inclose	unlike	expect
include	unwise	exchange
increase	uneasy	
indeed	untwist	**ex = egz**
injure	unjust	exact
injury	untie	exactly
inside	unknown	examine
inquire	until	example
incline	uproar	exist
intend	upset	exert

potato	habit	because
pocket	robin	carpet
palace	bridle	sharpen
shoulder	kitchen	alarm
Japan	complain	undone
Japanese	absent	cousin
parasol	curtain	Muffet
furrow	possible	money
burrow	linen	compare
sensible	graceful	quarrel
eleven	delay	scarlet
disease	certain	almond
animal	successful	prepare
blanket	market	uncover
frolic	discover	honey
dangerous	Monday	honeycomb
instead	depart	shovel
nobody	August	garden

Review of phonograms. The words are new.

advance	troublesome	lullaby
harness	comfortable	repair
company	among	awkward
parents	monkey	partridge
Santa Claus	reward	thousands

---

ph = f	pheasant	cipher
Philip	photograph	camphor
Philippine	phonics	nephew
Ralph	Joseph	elephant
telephone	orphan	alphabet
telegraph	sulphur	geography

---

gh = f	rough	enough
cough	roughest	laugh
coughing	tough	laughing
trough	toughen	laughter

---

mn = m	autumn	solemn
hymn	column	condemn

ch = k	chorus	schooner
ache	school	anchor
echo	scholar	orchestra
Christmas	scheme	stomach

---

ch = sh	chute	Champlain
Chicago	Charlotte	ruching

---

sc = s	scene	scissors
scent	scenery	scythe

---

i = y	brilliant	Spaniard
onion	opinion	Daniel
union	companion	warrior
million	Italian	familiar

---

i = long e	machine	**qu = k**
trio	ravine	conquer
marine	police	mosquito
magazine	valise	

di = j	**silent h**	Rhine
soldier	John	exhaust
	heir	
ti = ch	hour	**et = long a**
question	honor	bouquet
suggestion	honest	croquet
digestion	ghost	crochet

---

ce, ci, si, ti = sh		
	excursion	invitation
	permission	vacation
	action	notion
	collection	motion
	correction	promotion
ocean	objection	mention
musician	station	attention
physician	nation	intention
precious	combination	position
delicious	relation	condition
special	recitation	addition

important	diamonds	druggist
snowflakes	postage	valuable
snowbirds	gentlemen	yesterday
forbid	holiday	perfect
forsake	subtraction	remain
overload	twilight	direction
postpone	patient	parade
buttercups	mistletoe	electric
powerless	medicine	probably
president	fireman	farther
fastest	different	darling
to-day	post-office	forest
mistake	beneath	piano
oatmeal	underneath	pavement
excitement	messenger	costliest
snarl	janitor	to-morrow
railroad	unfold	anchor
lonesome	hundred	multiplication

Review of phonograms. The words are new.

SUGGESTIONS TO TEACHERS

Do not put this book into the hands of your pupils until you have carefully studied these suggestions.

The following plan approximates the progress of the average primary class. Do not attempt to follow it exactly. Keep in mind the fact that the ability of pupils differs greatly, and that whether a class falls behind the suggested plan of work or advances more rapidly, the one important thing is to teach each step thoroughly.

The amount of time given daily to the work in phonics must be decided by the teacher. Classroom conditions make it possible for some to give twenty minutes a day while others can give but ten. Two exercises a day of ten minutes each is perhaps the ideal arrangement. The exercise should never be continued until pupils weary of it. At the first indication of lagging or weariness it is time to stop.

The teaching of phonics includes

I Ear training,
II Tongue training,
III Eye training,
IV Word building.

Ear training may begin on the first day the child enters school. Say to the pupils, "We shall play a little game. You may do what I tell you, but do not speak a word." Then say to one, "Bring me a b-o-x," speaking the last word very slowly (phonetically); to others, "Show me something r-e-d," "Tap on your d-e-s-k," "Touch something made of t-i-n," "Cl-a-p your h-ands," "R-u-n to the d-oo-r," "H-o-p to the w-i-n-d-ow," etc. Sufficient interest will soon be aroused to *permit the* teacher to leave off the play and say words phonetically, one after another, asking pupils to tell what each word is. In a few days they will be able to recognize almost any word that may be sounded. Occasionally tell a little story, saying a word phonetically here and there, and allowing pupils to pronounce the word. This form of training may be profitably continued throughout the first half-year.

Tongue training should begin about the third or fourth day. Sound a word and have a pupil tell what sound he hears first, what sound he hears last. Be very careful that he gives the sound correctly. There is a natural inclination to voice a breath, or voiceless sound, such as *h*. Holding an object before a pupil have him say the name slowly (phonetically), as *h-a-t*, *c-a-p*, *v-a-s-e*, *p-e-n*, *b-oo-k*, *f-a-n*, etc. A picture may be placed before the class, and a pupil may be asked to say phonetically the name of each thing he sees in the picture. After a few days' practice offer a sound (it may be a simple phonogram, as *l*, or a compound phonogram, as *sl*); have the pupils see how many different words they can think of beginning with that sound. This training should be continued for several months. Ear training and tongue training should be practiced for eight or ten days before taking up eye training.

Eye training begins with the book, — teaching the pupil to associate the sound with the symbol. Ask the pupil to name the pictures on page 5; he says, *man*, *moon*. Ask him what sound he hears first (the ear and the tongue training have prepared the way for prompt recognition), and he will reply, *m*. Now tell him that the letters at the top of the page are pictures of the first sound and that hereafter they will help him to tell words. The pupil next learns the sound of *a*, in the same way. Then he learns the sound of *n*. Now he says the sounds of the three letters *m-a-n*, and thereby discovers the word *man*. At first the pupil will say these sounds so far apart that he cannot hear a word, but keep him trying to say them more rapidly, as, *m——a——n*, *m—a—n*, *m–a–n*, *m-a-n*, until he does hear the word and tells it. Proceed in like manner with the lessons that follow.

The order in which the phonograms are presented is based upon the ease with which they are blended.

In the early lessons tell the pupil only the sound of the letter that is illustrated. It is confusing to many pupils to be told the name of the letter at the same time that they are told its sound. Some teachers prefer not to teach the names of the letters until the pupils have worked on the sounds three or four months. Whenever a teacher feels sure that a pupil knows the sound of a letter so thoroughly that it will not confuse him to be told its name also, then it is time to teach him the name of the letter. It is not necessary for pupils to know the letters in alphabetical order until later.

The number of pages taken in a given lesson must be governed by the ability of the class. Take only as many as the pupils can do well.

During the first eight weeks pupils should have each lesson in both script and print. Write the lesson on the blackboard and have them practice it from that before practicing from the print in the book. By so doing, they will learn both forms simultaneously. As the lessons grow longer, limited time and blackboard space will prevent the teacher from presenting in script the whole of each day's work; but whenever a new phonogram or phonic principle is introduced, several of the words representing it should first be explained, sounded, and pronounced from the blackboard. Experience will soon enable the teacher to judge how much script practice is necessary to prepare the pupils for the book lesson.

This phonic course contains over 3500 different words. Each of these words when presented contains but one new phonogram, and that phonogram is the one introduced at the beginning of the series in which the word occurs.

Never tell the pupil a word in his phonic lesson, since only one new sound is introduced at a time, and the new step offers no difficulty if each foregoing page has been thoroughly learned.

When it is necessary to indicate a certain sound in a word, call it by number — the second sound, the third sound, or whatever it may be.

Concert recitation is helpful to timid pupils, and it saves time; but it should be avoided until the teacher is sure that each pupil participating in it can give the sound of every consonant correctly. The greater part of the phonic work should be individual.

Encourage pupils to whisper the sounds to themselves when they are studying a phonic or a reading lesson. Without actually hearing the sounds they cannot get the blend and therefore cannot discover the word. It takes several months for pupils to be able to blend the sounds mentally. This whispering is not disorder. It is a necessary part of word-getting and, if checked too soon, the pupils' progress in word-getting may be greatly retarded. When the proper time for overcoming it has arrived, — toward the latter part of the first year, — pupils will naturally dispense with it because they will be able to get the word so quickly through the eye that they will not wait for the assistance of the ear. An occasional request from the teacher that the pupil shall study to himself without moving the lips, will overcome it without difficulty.

Reserve a small space on the blackboard for a permanent phonic chart. As pupils learn the sounds of the consonants, write them at the left in this space; and as each new compound phonogram is learned, write it at the right. This affords good material for reviews and word-building lessons conducted in the following way: The teacher points to a consonant, then to a compound phonogram, and pupils tell what word these would make if written together; or a pupil takes the pointer and indicates combinations that will make familiar words while either he or other pupils pronounce them.

After all of its phonograms have been presented, the script alphabet should be placed along the top of the blackboard, and under each letter should be given the corresponding letter printed on paper or pasteboard. If it is on pasteboard it may be pinned to the blackboard; if on paper, paste it with library paste — it can easily be washed off when necessary. This affords ready reference for the entire class, familiarizing them with both the script and the printed forms. Do not print on the blackboard. The printing never looks exactly as it does in the book. Reserve the blackboard for script.

No diacritical marks are to be used. Pupils are taught to determine the sound of the vowel by its position in the word and by its associate letters. When pupils learn to read by means of diacritical marks their reading for the first year or more must be largely confined to the reader from which they are taught. The method presented in this book gives the pupil immediate mastery of a word taught and the words of its family, regardless of where he may find them. Diacritical marks should not be taught until pupils are sufficiently advanced to use the dictionary.

Pupils should be taxed with the fewest possible rules. In this course only those are used which are simplest and most necessary for word-recognition. Do not require pupils to memorize them; frequent application of the principles involved will insure a thorough knowledge of them.

The separation of the family name from the initial sound greatly assists the pupil in acquiring the "blend." It becomes less necessary and is therefore used less frequently as the work proceeds. Strive for the "blend" at all times. The pupil's power to discover new words depends upon his ability to blend the sounds of which they are composed.

Constantly require pupils to apply their knowledge of phonics to their reading lesson; that is, do not tell the pupil a word *in his reading* lesson which he is able to get for himself. The habit of "making the sounds tell the word" must be thoroughly fixed. Thus the pupil will daily become more self-helpful, and after a few months his general knowledge of phonics will enable him to recognize many words containing sounds beyond his phonic training.

When a word occurs in the reading lesson that does not conform to the rule, as, *have*, *give*, etc., and the pupil pronounces it incorrectly, ask him if he knows such a word; when he replies that he does not, tell him there is something wrong with his vowel. He will immediately correct it and will soon learn to expect "exceptions," and to try another sound of a letter if his first sounding does not give him a familiar word, or a word that "makes sense" in the context.

If a word unusually long yet containing only sounds previously taught occurs in the reading lesson and seems difficult for the pupil, assist him by writing it on the blackboard and underscoring each compound phonogram or family name; also teach him to put a finger over such a word, moving it off slowly so that he sees but one family name or one syllable at a time. This may be well demonstrated to the class by using a long narrow strip of pasteboard with which to cover the word on the blackboard and removing it in the way described above. With a little training pupils will soon learn to do this and will find it very helpful.

When the teacher discovers a weakness in a phonic principle previously taught, she should promptly refer the pupil or the class to a lesson which demonstrates that principle. If it is a forgotten phonogram, the pupil should be given a quick review of the family of words in which that phonogram is the common element.

Make up sets of script phonic cards for seat work. Write four or five families in as many columns on each card. Write the initial consonant sound in red ink and the compound phonogram or family name in black. Again write the consonant sounds in red on strips of pasteboard and on other strips write the family names in black. Cut these strips up so that there is but one consonant or one family name on each card. Pupils use these small cards for building families of words to correspond with those on the large card. Keep the small cards and the corresponding large one in the same envelope. When desired, the pupils may use the large cards for study or for copying. Each large card should be numbered on the back to correspond with the number of the envelope in which it belongs. Write on the outside of the envelope the name of each family included in the envelope; then it will not be necessary to look into the envelope in order to know what work the envelope contains.

When pupils have had a few weeks' practice in writing, begin conducting phonic spelling lessons, in order to reinforce the power to recognize compound phonograms. Write a family name on the blackboard, as, *at;* write it several times, one under another, making a column; now pronounce this family of words,—*cat*, *bat*, *fat*, *hat*, *mat*, *rat*, *pat*, *sat*, requiring different pupils to go to the blackboard and prefix the sound which makes the word. Or write on the blackboard the compound phonogram which is to be the common element of the series, then have the pupils copy it on their paper. Now pronounce the words, having children write as the words are pronounced. The ability to recognize compound phonograms as wholes, without separating them into their elementary sounds, greatly shortens the process of word recognition. This also serves to impress phonic principles upon the minds of the pupils and teaches them to apply those principles to all spelling, thus making spelling a matter of reasoning. Pupils should be taught to look over a spelling lesson, when one has been assigned that is made up of words of different families, and to determine the "dangerous places" *in the words.* For instance, in a spelling lesson of ten words, seven of those words may be strictly phonetic; that is, they may be governed by phonic principles and be spelled as they sound. The pupil does not need to waste time on these. But in the remaining three he finds unphonetic elements, so he studies only those three "exceptions." It is a good plan, in teaching children how to do this, to write the spelling lesson on the blackboard, making in red chalk the letters on which pupils are likely to trip. Some teachers have aptly called these "red danger signals."

If the pupils are taking up this course in the fall after having had part of the work the previous year, they should take a rapid review of the pages up to the point where their new lessons begin.

When pupils enter the class from schools in which this phonic course has not been taught, the most satisfactory method of preparing them for work with the class is to take them rapidly over the work which the class has covered.

Whether pupils complete this course in one year, one and a half, or two years, when they have completed it their ability to read anything they can comprehend is assured. Each pupil should keep the course in his desk for ready reference, general reviews, and drills, as required, until the close of his third school year.

The words in this book are grouped according to their pronunciation in Webster's New International Dictionary.

LIST OF PHONOGRAMS STUDIED

WITH PAGE REFERENCES

RULES

NOT EXEMPLIFIED IN THE LIST ABOVE